TAMU PETRA BROWNE

Principles of Business Management Study Guide 1

TAMU PETRA BROWNE

Principles of Business Management

Study Guide 1

© Tamu Petra Browne
Bird Rock • PO Box 890
Basseterre, St. Kitts
www.tamubrowne.webs.com • Email managementofbusiness@gmail.com

Table of Contents

Introduction

Welcome to this dynamic subject where theories come to life every day around us. Management of Business is an exciting subject and the skills learnt here can be transferred even in one's daily life. The World Wide Web has given us insight into the inner workings of businesses at our fingertips, often in real time, providing up to the minute information on global events in the business world.

This guide will seek to expose you to the major business concepts in a simple yet engaging manner. It will provide Internet and traditional textbook resources that will allow for in depth study of key concepts. The guide will also feature news stories and articles that will help clarify and illustrate business and management at work in the real world. You will also have the ability to test your knowledge. Readers enjoy, it is time to sharpen your business skills and begin the journey that will take you from student to CEO.

Look out for these symbols throughout this guide.

ICON KEY

- File this Away
- Test your knowledge
- Web resources
- Challenges

File Away are special notes about a topic, such as exception to the theory or some concept that is particularly important.

Test your Knowledge are the many ways you can determine how well you understand the concepts outlined. Knowledge testing may include essays, structured questions, multiple choice questions and case studies.

Web resources will point you to material on the Internet that will assist in your understanding of certain concepts under study.

Challenges will do just that, challenge you to look at a business concept in a new light or from an entirely different perspective to the norm.

What will this guide cover?

This guide will cover the following major areas:

1. **Business and its Environment.**

2. **The Management of People.**

3. **Business Finance and Accounting.**

Business and its Environment

W hat you need to know

1. The types of business activity.

2. The different types of private sector and public sector organizations and their advantages and disadvantages.

3. The different types of economic systems and their impact on a firm's size and growth.

4. Measures of a firm's size. Advantages and disadvantages of large and small firms.

5. Ethics and decision making.

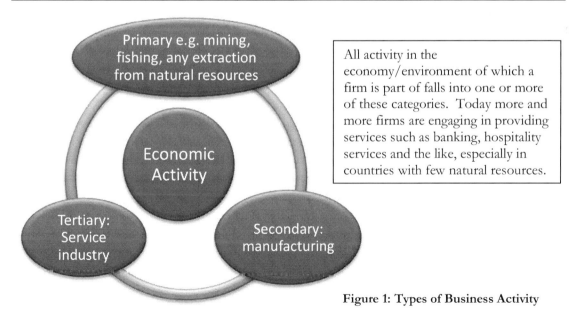

All activity in the economy/environment of which a firm is part of falls into one or more of these categories. Today more and more firms are engaging in providing services such as banking, hospitality services and the like, especially in countries with few natural resources.

Figure 1: Types of Business Activity

Figure 1.1 Legal Structures of Businesses

Private Sector

Sole trader

- single owner invests all the capital, has full control and reaps all profits but bears all losses.

Partnerships

- Two or more persons working together to run the business. They share all profits and losses.

Private Limited Companies

- Have Ltd after their names.Ownership is in the form of shares issued by the original owner to family,friends and sometimes employees. Shares are not sold on the stock exchange. Shares can only be sold with the agreement of other shareholders

Public Limited Companies

- Have plc or inc after their names. Shares are sold on the stock exchange. Sahreholders can sell and buy shares from anyone.

Co-operatives

- found often in the agriculture industry. All members own and run the business. All members have an equal vote and all share the profits.

Franchises

- The franchisor sells his business model. The franchisee gets the business name, marketing material and epertise, training and support from the franchisor. eg KFC, Subway.

Joint ventures

- These business partnerships exist for the sole purpose of executing a particular project. two or more business entities. All parties share in profits and losses.

Public Sector

Public Corporations

- Owned and run by the state. Provides social goods. Profit is not a motive.

Statutory Bodies

- public entity contolled by a Board on behalf of Government. Profit is a motive.

All firms exist in either the public or private sector. Public sector firms are owned and managed by Government, while private sector firms are run by private individuals like you. Each business formation has its own unique advantages and disadvantages.

- 📁 Limited companies differ from partnerships and sole traders in 3 ways.
- 📁 Limited liability i.e. the only liability a shareholder has is limited to the amount of his shares.
- 📁 Legal Personality i.e. these companies are separate legally from their owners. These companies can be sued separately from their owners.
- 📁 Continuity i.e. if the owner dies the business will still continue through its shareholders and an appointment of a new manager.

 Challenge!
Think about a business you would like to start and determine which is the best legal formation for that business and why.

Disadvantages and Advantages of Business Organizations

Table 1: Sole trader Organizations

Advantages	Disadvantages
No legalities to set up	Unlimited liability-all owners property at risk if losses occur
Owner has complete control	Owner may not have sufficient expertise in all areas e.g. accounting, marketing
Owner shares profits with no one	Owner assumes all losses.
The business is often the passion of the owner	Raising capital to start/expand is quite difficult.
One on one customer care	No continuity-when owner dies business closes

Table 2: Partnerships

Advantages	Disadvantages
Partners share in the business' losses	Partners must share the business' profits
Easier to raise capital	Cannot raise capital through shares
Fewer legal formalities to set up than a company	Unlimited liability
The business is often the passion of the owner	Conflict may arise in decision making
Partners may have different expertise to lend	No continuity when a partner dies

Table 3: Private Limited Company

Advantages	Disadvantages
All shareholders have limited liability	Many legal formalities to create the company
Ability to raise capital through issue of shares	Shares can only be sold when other shareholders agree
Separate legal personality	Shares only sold to a select few
Original owner can maintain control through majority shares	Raising capital to start/expand is quite difficult.
	Continuity if a shareholder dies

🗀 Legal steps to form a company include:
Memorandum of Association: company name and contact info, aim of firm, and maximum share capital.

🗀 Articles of Association: Names the Board of Directors, procedure at Board Meetings

Table 4: Public Limited Company

Advantages	Disadvantages
Limited liability	Legal formalities to set up business
Easy to raise large amounts of capital through share issue	Risk of takeover since shares traded on Stock Exchange
Continuity	Share prices may fluctuate due to external shocks
Easy to trade shares	Management and shareholders may be in conflict
One on one customer care	Full disclosure of company accounts

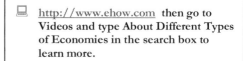
Business and the Economic Environment

There are four main types of economic systems in which firms exist. The subsistence economy involves persons only producing enough to meet their own needs. There is no surplus for export. This is also known as a traditional economy.

A planned economy often exists in socialist states, where all commercial activity is administered and planned by government. In this economic system the government controls and regulates the production, distribution and pricing.

The free market economy is a mainly theoretical concept, where all resources are allocated only on supply and demand in the marketplace. In this type of economic system there are no government regulations whatsoever. Even capitalist countries such as the United States have some degree of governmental regulations to govern trade.

A mixed economy is the economic system that most firms exist in today. It is comprised of both public sector and private sector firms.

💣 Do some research to determine the impact of the above economic systems on a business' size and growth.

How do you measure a company's size?

- Number of employees: generally the more employees the larger the company.
- Output/Sales: The greater the quantity produced or the higher the sales figure often the larger the company.
- Market share: The higher the firm's capture of the market, generally the larger the firm.
  - Total sales of firm/Total sales of industry x 100
- Market capitalization: This measure is only used for publically traded firms. The higher the capitalization i.e. the value of a firm's shares the larger the size.
  - Current share price X Total number of shares issued.
  - Share prices fluctuate so not often a stable measure.
- Capital employed: larger firms tend to have more capital invested. However small firms may e more capital intensive than larger ones. For instance a sole trader – a dentist will have a large amount of capital employed as the equipment in use is quite expensive.

> 📁 These measures are not entirely fool proof but are general measures. Often more than one measure must be used to determine the size of a company.

Big or small that is the question?

- It is easier for larger firms to raise capital.
- Larger firms have greater economies of scale – the more units produced the lower the cost per unit.
- Larger firms have more options and opportunity for growth.
- Managers can exert more control of smaller firms.
- Smaller firms have the opportunity to provide more one on one customer service.

How can Businesses Grow?

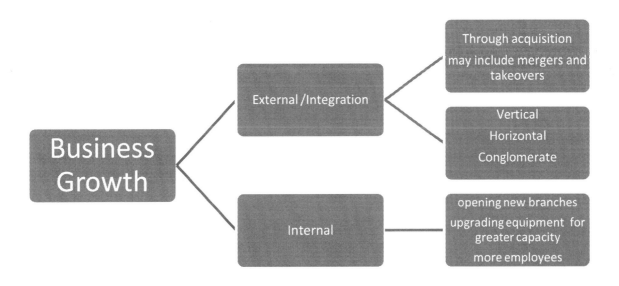

http://businesscasestudies.co.uk/ Then go to Revision Theory and search for Growth

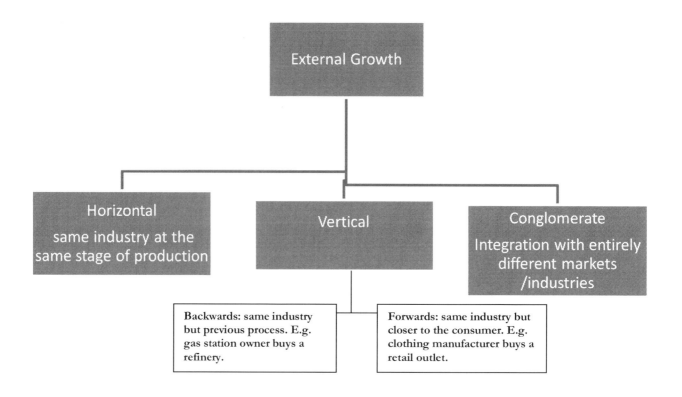

Table 5: Types of integration and their advantages and disadvantages

Type of Integration	Advantages	Disadvantages
Horizontal	Reduces competition in the industry	Monopolies can be created which may result in higher prices for the consumer.
	Can bargain more with suppliers	
	May lead to economies of scale.	
Vertical Backward	Control over frequency, pricing, reliability and quality of supply to themselves and competitors.	May not have adequate expertise in the new business.
Vertical Forward	Firms can now control the pricing and promotion of its products	Inadequate expertise.
	Ensures a guaranteed sales outlet for products.	
Conglomerate	Diversification which spreads risk.	Lack of expertise in a new industry.
		Loss of focus and muddled goals and objectives.

💣 Is rapid growth always positive? Research the internet for case studies about firms' growing pains. This will help you in determining the advantages and disadvantages of rapid growth.

🗁 The main problems resulting from rapid growth fit into the following categories.
🗁 Financial
🗁 Managerial
🗁 Promotion/marketing
🗁 Loss of control

Business Objectives and Decision Making

Whether a business is a large or small one, whether it is engaged in rapid growth or not, all businesses must have objectives that focus their day to day and long term activities and decisions.

A business' objectives are those targets it wishes to achieve. All objectives must be **S.M.A.R.T- Specific, Measurable, Achievable, Relevant and Timely.**

Hierarchy of Business Objectives

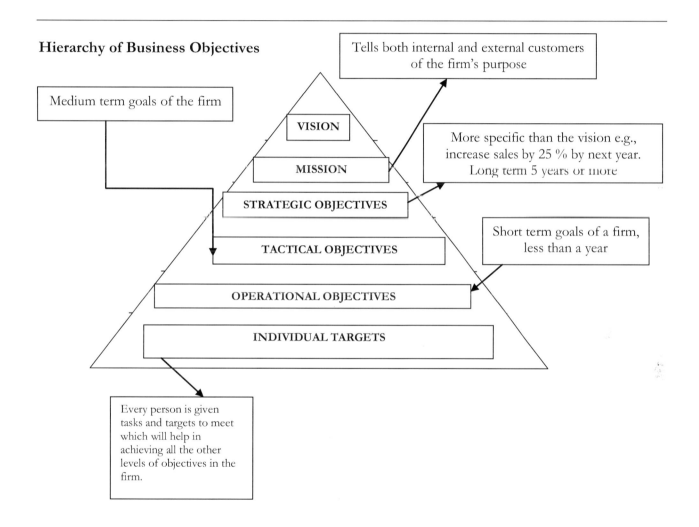

Tells both internal and external customers of the firm's purpose

Medium term goals of the firm

VISION

MISSION

More specific than the vision e.g., increase sales by 25 % by next year. Long term 5 years or more

STRATEGIC OBJECTIVES

TACTICAL OBJECTIVES

Short term goals of a firm, less than a year

OPERATIONAL OBJECTIVES

INDIVIDUAL TARGETS

Every person is given tasks and targets to meet which will help in achieving all the other levels of objectives in the firm.

Question: What is the difference between a vision statement and a mission statement?

Explain THREE reasons why mission statements are important.

Visit:
http://www.diffen.com/difference/Mission_Statement_vs_Vision_Statement

What you need to know about Business Objectives

- Objectives can be strategic (long term, more than five years), medium term (tactical) and short term/operational (within a year).
- There are some common business objectives including
    - **Profit maximization.** –this is the reason for entering the marketplace.
    - **Growth** – businesses want to grow to increase revenue and profit.
    - **Increase the firm's share of the market.**
    - **Survival** – this is usually an objective when the firm is first established.
    - **Ethical and social responsibility** – more and more firms are placing social responsibility and ethics on their objective list. Ethics are principles to ensure honest conduct while doing business. Social responsibility refers to the management of a business' processes and end product so that it has a net positive impact on the society in which it exists.

    🖳 http://www.futurity.org/society-culture/workplace-ethics-rub-off-on-employees/ **to read about ethics in the workplace.**

    💣 **Research a company that has shown commendable social responsibility.**

    💣 **Research the term Good Corporate Governance.**

Why are Business Objectives Important?

- They focus the direction of employees.
- They provide the basis for evaluation. A firm needs to set goals and then compare its performance against them to determine its progress.
- They aid in resource allocation. Firms will allocate more resources to areas that are necessary to the achievement of their objectives.
- They help to motivate workers.

💣 **Set some personal objectives of your own. Create TWO Strategic, TWO Tactical and TWO Operational objectives for yourself. Remember to make them SMART! Also remember that your tactical and operational objectives must help you achieve your strategic objectives.**

Decision Making

Managers make scores of decisions every day, often to advance their firm's objectives. Sound decisions must be made to avoid losses and secure profits for the company. Decision making is the process used to arrive at the solution to a problem. There are two types of decisions managers generally make:

Programmed and Non-programmed Decisions

- **Programmed decisions** – are routine and tend to be repetitive. There are often company policies, procedures or rules to deal with such. Managers have all the information required to make the decision. Solution is clear. E.g. what should a manger do after an employee is late three times? The solution to this is in the Employee Handbook as this problem occurs often and regularly.

- **Non-programmed decisions** – required when problems are new, and the information is incomplete or ambiguous. E.g. what is the best strategy to advertise a new product in a new market? All the information is not available.

- Information used in the decision making process should be **accurate, timely, relevant and cost effective**.

The Decision Making Process
It is often felt that managers make decisions based on intuition formed through experiences in the business world. Although intuition is factored into many decisions manager make, most successful managers use a rational decision making process.

Process
1. **Definition of the problem** – this involves identifying the core issue that is to be solved.

2. **Data collection and analysis** – deciding what type of research is required – primary or secondary and looking for patterns in the research.

3. **Generation of alternative solutions**

4. **Selection of best alternative** – sometimes criteria is used to determine the alternative, factors such as cost may be considered.

5. **Implementation and evaluation** - the resources are allocated to put the solution into action. The results after implementation are reviewed to determine if the appropriate decision was made.

Factors impacting the decision making process

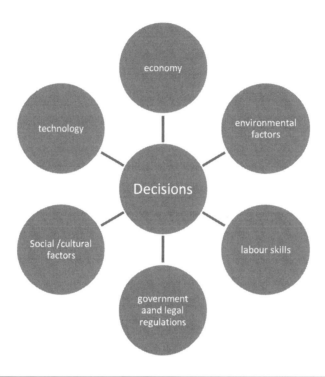

Decision Making Tools

There are qualitative and quantitative factors that must be considered in the decision making process.

- Qualitative factors are not numerical based and often take into account human and other intangible elements. Management needs to consider a decision's impact on its SWOT (Strengths, Weaknesses, Opportunities, and Threats), Human Resource Management (morale, motivation) and on stakeholders (employees, customers, suppliers, citizens).

- Quantitative factors provide a numerical basis for decision making. May include forecasted sales and output figures, market share etc. A combination of both qualitative and quantitative factors is most often used to make decisions. E.g. critical path analysis; decision tree; cost benefit analysis.

Question

You have to choose a university at which to pursue your Bachelor's Degree. You are determined to enrich your university experience and so you have decided to go to one outside the country where you currently live. You have narrowed it down to three schools in three different countries. Use the rational decision making process to determine which of the three schools you will attend.

Critical Path Method www.netmba.com/operations/project/cpm/

The critical path method/analysis is a project management technique that aids mangers in their scheduling of activities that comprise a project the diagram is a visual representation that shows the sequence and duration of the activities required to complete a project. The length of the project is estimated by the critical path. Activities along this critical path (longest path) cannot be delayed without delaying the entire project.

The circles stand for events, the arrows for activities. The name of the activity and its duration label each arrow/activity. You number the nodes(circles) in order of completion.

All activies with NO preceeding activity begin at node 1.

Activity	Precedence	Duration
	Happens before the activity	days
A	-	3
B	A	8
C	-	7
D	-	12
E	B,D	10
F	C,E	20

The critical path is the longest path to completion and is **D,E,F (12+10+20) = 42 DAYS. These activities cannot run late and are critical to the project's completion.**

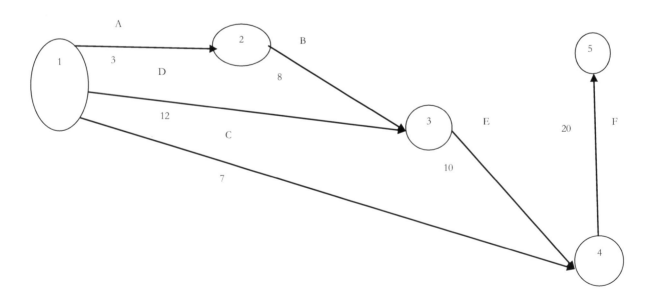

Calculating Event Times

- Earliest Event Times/Earliest Start Times – EST for an event occurs when all activities leading into that event are complete. The EST and LFT of Node 1 always equals zero. EST for A =0, B=(0+3)=3, C=(3+12+10)=22. You take the preceding EST and add the next task's duration. When there is more than one activity entering a node you chose the longest activity to continue computing EST.

- Latest Finish Times (LFT) for events are calculated by determining the latest it can occur without delaying subsequent events. To find LFTs, work backwards through the network from the finish node to the start node. When there is more than one activity entering a node you chose the longest activity to continue computing LFT. The LFT of the final node is always equal to its EST, so you take that LFT and subtract the durations.

- The Node is divided in half and the EST is placed in the top right corner and LFT at the bottom.

- Calculate the ESTs and LFTs of the above critical path diagram.

Node	EST	LFT
1	0 first node always is zero	0 (12 -12) longer duration to get to node 1
2	3 (0+3) previous EST +duration	4 (12-8)
3	12 (0+12) longer duration	12 (22-10)
4	22 (12+10) longer duration	22 (42-20) LST - duration
5	42 (22+20)	42 always same as last EST

- Dummy activities are inserted into critical path diagrams to make the diagram more coherent. No time or other resources are spent on these activities. They are shown by a dotted line. They have no duration.

- Float time/slack time-is spare time available to complete an activity. It is the time that can be delayed on an activity without delaying the entire project. **Total float= LFT – EFT.**

Decision Trees: A decision tree is yet another graphical representation of the decisions and monetary outcomes of making specific decisions. It presents all the alternatives available to a manager and the monetary value attached to each one.

Case Study:
Tammy has been running her own spa for five years and her clientele is growing. She wants to add some new facial services. To do this though she will need added space, and has consulted a contractor. She has found out that a 500 sq foot expansion will be adequate but not her ideal space and that double that size would be ideal. Tammy is facing increasing competition to her business from a number of spa franchises, who have savvy advertising and many more small proprietors. She forecasts that there is a 60% probability that her 500 sq ft property will yield her a pay off $50,000 and a 40% chance that she might make $85,000 more because of competition by larger spas. The larger spa she forecasts will give her a 70% chance of making $80,000 in profit and there is only a 30% chance she will make $30,000. Construct a decision tree and determine which option Tammy should choose.

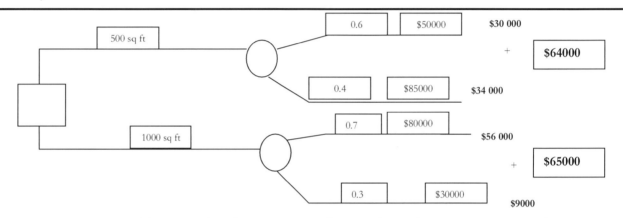

The alternative Tammy should choose is based on the Expected Value of each alternative. The expected value is calculated by multiplying each probability by the expected pay off and adding the ones that come off of the same chance node. See the expected values in **bold print** above. The highest Expected Value is $65,000 and as such Tammy's decision should be to build the 1000 sq ft expansion.

Let us suppose costs were involved. Let us say it cost $10,000 to build the 500 sq ft addition and $17,000 to build the 1000 square foot property. You would deduct the costs from the expected values to arrive at the net profit and choose the option with the highest net profit. In this example the net profit of the 500 sq ft space is ($64000-$10,000) =$54,000. The net profit of the 1000 sq ft space is ($65000-$17000) = $48,000. So we would now change our decision and build the 500 sq ft addition.

What you need to know about Decision Trees

- It is constructed from left to right. The squares are decision points and are called decision nodes.

- The circles show what outcomes can occur and are called chance nodes.

- All branches leaving a chance node has a probability. All probabilities from a chance node must add up to one.

Cost Benefit Analysis

💻 http://management.about.com

Type in Cost Benefit Analysis. Select the first result to learn more

This is a quantitative tool that is used to advise management on whether or not a certain decision should be taken. The benefits/positive factors and costs/negative factors are quantified and the costs deducted from the benefits. If the result is positive the decision can be taken. If there is more than one alternative the one with the highest positive net value should be chosen.

Tool	Advantages	Disadvantages
Critical Path Analysis	Assists in the management of time and allocation of resources. Assists in monitoring cash flow. Knowing the critical path prevents delay.	Usefulness limited in large, complex projects. Needs clear and reliable information to be accurate. Requires managerial competence to determine event times etc.
Decision Trees	Allows for clarity in decision making. Probability allows for flexibility. Relatively easy to construct.	Uses a number of estimates of pay offs and probabilities etc. If these are inaccurate so too will be the decision. Needs qualitative data to inform the quantitative data and give a true picture
Cost Benefit Analysis	Simple to determine the final answer. Takes into account societal costs and benefits.	Much of the benefits/costs are not easily quantifiable.

Multinational Corporations

Businessdictionary.com defines a Multinational Corporation (MNC) as an "enterprise operating in several countries but managed from one (home) country. Generally, any firm or group that derives a quarter of its revenue from operations outside of its home country is considered a MNC." Examples of MNCs include Coca Cola, Marriott, Four Seasons Resort, Cadbury and Kellogg.

🖝 The presence of multinationals in the Caribbean and other parts of the world has been part of Government strategy to increase the size, diversity and profitability of their tourism sectors. Many Caribbean Governments are actively pursuing a tourism based and hospitality services based economy and are moving away from traditional agriculture based economies.

Table 6: Advantages and Disadvantages of Multinational Corporations

Advantages	Disadvantages
Increases foreign exchange reserves	Most of the profits repatriated to MNC's home country
Increased employment opportunities for local population	Crime and environmental degradation often increases
Multiplier effect as other businesses benefit e.g. taxi drivers, farmers etc.	Influence of Western culture on host country/dilution of host country's cultural identity.
Tax revenues to government	Criticized as a new form of colonialism/jobs are often low paying and menial in nature
MNCs experience economies of scale, lower production and often labour costs.	Small firms may not be able to compete and so the number of local businesses is reduced.

Why have multinationals grown

- Improvement in transportation and hence distribution systems. Trade liberalization and globalization Improvements in technology and communication systems.

Trade Liberalization and Globalization

Trade Liberalization is the removal of barriers to trade. Barriers include tariffs (duties, export subsidies) and non-tariff barriers to trade (licensing, quotas, standards such as labeling). The removal of these barriers, are to encourage what is known as free trade amongst countries.

The introduction of trade liberalization has removed the practice of protectionism, where governments sought to protect their domestic economies by the implementation of those barriers to trade mentioned above. Those in favor of liberalization, point to an increase in consumption choices and encourages more international trade. They argue that increased trade will allow all countries involved in free trade to make more money. Persons against trade liberalization argue that asking smaller, lesser developed countries to open their borders to free trade puts them at a disadvantage, as larger countries flood their markets with cheaper goods, with which local businesses cannot compete due to their lack of economies of scale.

> ⌨ **The World Trade Organization (WTO) is the body that governs international free trade. Visit www.wto.org to learn more.**

> ⌨ **Visit my YouTube channel managementofbusiness for videos on globalization and trade liberalization.**

Globalization: Visit www.gobalization101.org to learn more

Globalization is a cultural, social and economic phenomenon. It involves the deepening of relationships and increasing connectivity amongst countries around the globe. It can be defined as the growing interdependence amongst nation states their organizations and people.

Globalization has been fueled by trade liberalization, technology, telecommunication, government legislation and policy agendas to encourage globalization such as tax free holidays and economic citizenship. There has also been greater globalization due to travel, education and widening of consumer tastes and preferences, along with improvements in transportation.

Globalization's positive impacts include:

- A wider market for firms' goods and services

- Reduced costs of production as firms source inputs from or locate in territories with lower cost structures.

- There is also wider choice for consumers as goods and services can be ordered through ecommerce from almost anywhere on the globe. Consumers also have to assume more responsibility and research their purchases.

- The transfer of technology and knowledge also occur.

Globalization's negative impacts include:

- Increased competition – local firms that are smaller and less able to compete may be forced out of the market.

- Brain drain – as persons with education and skills sought after such as those in the nursing profession emigrate for better opportunities.

- Local markets are flooded with low cost goods – firms from larger countries may have lower overheads and benefit from economies of scale, which reduce their production costs. This cost savings is then passed onto the consumer, thus pricing domestic firms out of the market. Economies of scale occur when firms produce large amounts of output their average unit cost is reduced. For instance a firm with costs of $1000 that produces 10 items has an average unit cost of 1000/10 which is $100 per item. However, when that firm increases its production to 1000 units its unit cost falls to 1000/1000, $1 per item.

- Firms that engage in globalization by locating in other territories will also now need to adopt international human resource practices which are often quite complex and may require significant training of current staff.

💣 Challenge yourself to write a brief discussion on the following:

Explain the relationship between trade liberalization and globalization (8 marks)

Discuss THREE impacts of globalization on developing countries. (15 marks)

Management of People

All managers whether their businesses are large or small must view their employees as resources, human resources and seek to ensure that they are using them as efficiently as possible.

Management Theories

There have been quite a number of great thinkers in this field that have put forward theories that speak to role of employees in the success of any business, and how managers should function to achieve maximum profitability.

Classical Theory

This school of thought came about during the Industrial revolution when managers of factories were attempting to find the "one best way" to perform and manage tasks in order to ensure efficiency and standardisation.

Classical Theorists – Major contributors

Frederick Taylor – known as the "father of scientific management" sought to scientifically measure the optimum time to perform tasks in an industrial setting. These times then became standards against which performance could be measured.

Henry Gantt – He was an associate of Frederick Taylor and introduced the Gantt chart, a project management tool that tracks projects' progress in terms of work completed, work in progress and work to be done and is widely used today.

Frank and Lillian Gilbreth – a husband and wife team who conducted **motion studies.** They studied the actual motions/movements of the most productive workers of specific tasks and attempted to document the most efficient motions for performing a task. This led to standardization.

Henri Fayol – He is also classified in the Administrative school of thought as well. Fayol was the first to introduce the concept that managers had specific functions and said that management consisted of planning, organizing, commanding/leading, co-ordinating and controlling. Fayol also introduced the idea that there were fourteen key management principles including division of work, discipline, authority and unity of command and direction.

> 🖥 Visit www.12manage.com then type "Henri Fayol" in the search box to learn more about his fourteen principles of management.

Evaluation of Classical Management school of thought

The Classical thinkers contributed much to current day management practices. Contributions include the concept of division of work, specialization and standardization, division of management and workers. They are greatly criticized though for seeing workers as mere tools to achieve profitability. Additionally, classical theorists also advocated autocratic leadership – the idea that employees suggestions and ideas were not included in the decision making process, they also treated all firms and employees as homogenous/same.

Human Relations Theory

> 🖥 Visit www.netmba.com type "Theory X" in the search box to learn more.

The Human Relations movement introduced the idea for the first time that employees worked best when the felt appreciated by their supervisors, and that managers be trained to gain employees' co-operation and hence increase productivity.

The Hawthorne Studies of 1924 to 1932 which were conducted by Western Electric made a significant contribution to the Human Relations school of thought. The Study originally set out to determine how the level of lighting affected productivity. Instead the researchers found that it was not lighting that affected productivity (unless the illumination was so low workers were unable to see). They found that workers produced more based on their attitude towards management – a more favourable attitude yielded greater productivity. This became known as the **Hawthorne Effect**. The concept of organizational behavior came out of these studies as it was found that the behavior by managers and workers and their interaction affected productivity a much as the technical aspects of the job.

Douglas Mc Gregor's Theory X and Theory Y

Mc Gregor found that in the field of management there were two prevailing sets of thoughts about workers which he characterized as Theory X and Y.

Theory X	Theory Y
Assumes that workers are by nature lazy and dislike work	Workers are creative, like responsibility and often seek it out
Autocratic leadership must be used to ensure productivity. Workers must be closely supervised.	Mangers must strive to create some degree of autonomy/freedom, provide a challenging and stimulating work environment to ensure productivity.
There must be strict set of rules and policies. A clear rewards and punishment system in order to control employees.	Decision making should be decentralized and employees must have the tools to effectively carry out their jobs.
	Work was as natural as rest or play

Mc Gregor said that managers could view employee motivation from either of these theories. Mc Gregor realized that **Theory X** might be necessary as not all employees might have the maturity of **Theory Y** workers and so needed more control. However, this type of centralized and autocratic type of leadership may demotivate employees. **Theory Y** presents many opportunities for motivation including: delegation, job enlargement, inclusion in decision making and the use of performance appraisals. **Theory Y** implies that management's role is to provide a working environment that fosters innovation, initiative and flexibility.

Systems Theory

This theory states that the organization can e likened to the human body or any other system, where the focus is how the various parts of the system, i.e. the various departments and divisions work together as a whole (the firm). It focuses on the relationship and interdependence between parts and is a holistic way of looking at an organization. This theory also advocates that organizations must be open systems and most receive stimulus (information etc) from its environment or it will become obsolete and die – a condition known as **entropy**.

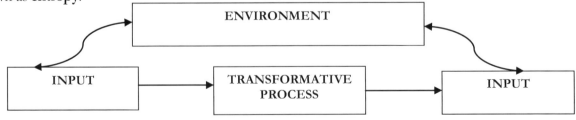

Organisation Structures

An organization's structure is its internal layout often illustrated in an organizational chart. The structure lets everyone know who is in charge, who reports to whom and what divisions and departments comprise the company.

Key elements in a structure include:

- **Hierarchy** – the levels in an organization – the more levels the "taller" the structure. Firms with less levels of management are known as "flat" and tend to be more responsive to change.

- **Chain of Command** – this shows how authority is passed down. Who is the boss, the supervisor etc and who is in charge of whom.

- **Span of control** – this indicates how many persons a manager is in charge of. Managers with many subordinates have a **wide** span of control, while those with few subordinates have a **narrow** span of control.

- **Centralization vs. decentralization** – this is the degree to which managers make all the decisions and delegate tasks. The more decision making is concentrated in one part of the organization such as in the top management level the ore centralized the structure is. The more managers delegate decision making and authority the more decentralized the firm is.

Types of structures

Figure 2: Functional Organization Structure

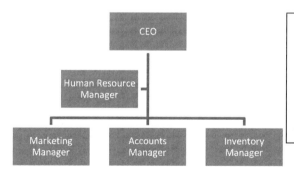

This structure divides the company into major products/divisions or geographical location, where each division has its own set of functional departments. E.g. an electronics manufacturer may have computer, television and stereo departments. Another company may structure their company around location such as North-East Division, Western Division etc.

- Company organized in departments. Employees placed in departments according to their similar roles.
- It allows for ease of resource allocation, supervision and co-ordination.
- Employees have a high degree of specialization.
- Communication between departments is often inefficient.
- Centralization of decision making.
- Managers often become focused on the needs of their department and lose focus of overall objectives.

Figure 3: Product/Divisional Structure

- Decentralized in nature thus flexible and responsive to change. Focus on market segment.
- Encourages innovation in divisions and of products.
- Communication between divisions is often inefficient. Unhealthy competition amongst divisions.
- Duplication of resources
- May lose sight of overall company objectives.

Figure 4: Matrix Structure

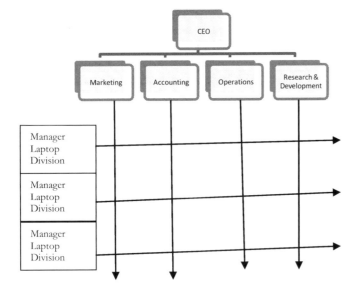

Matrix combines both the functional and the divisional structures. Each employee has two bosses.

- Effective for project based companies and multinationals.
- Allows for more efficient communication.
- Decentralised decision making.
- Employees often face conflicting sense of responsibility because of dual authority structure.
- Sharing of resources including time and human resources.
- Enhances co-operation and problem solving.
- Better customer service and performance accountability

Figure 5: Team Structure

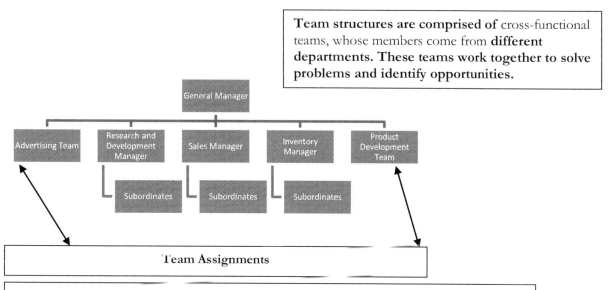

Team structures are comprised of cross-functional teams, whose members come from **different departments. These teams work together to solve problems and identify opportunities.**

Barriers between departments are reduced so better communication.

• Decision-making and response times speed up.

• Employees are motivated by enriching project oriented work.

• Levels of managers are eliminated so company more responsive to change.

Conflicting loyalties among team members as they report to team leaders and their department managers

Time-management issues arise as employees balance team and department goals

Increased time spent in meeting

The Network structure allows companies to outsource many of their major tasks. Employees at the hub or core communicate with the other companies that provide these critical services and hire specialist companies to perform key tasks. This type of organizational structure:
- Provides flexibility
- Reduces overhead cost as staff size is reduced.
- May have variable supply and quality as radial companies are not under control of the company.

Figure 6: Network Structure

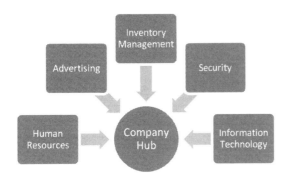

Organizational Design

The type of organization structure that a company chooses is influenced by a variety of factors.

- Degree of centralization/control required – certain industries and businesses require tight controls such as security firms, hence an organizational structure that fosters centralization would be most appropriate.

- Management style – the more autocratic managers are the more control they desire and would choose an organization structure that enables them to exercise such control.

- Adoption of technology – as businesses adopt more information technology, this reduces the need for as many employees as automation makes work easier. This will lead to de-layering i.e. the reduction in middle management, thus generally the more automation – the flatter the organizational structure.

An effective organization structure should have the following characteristics:

- Encourage growth and development

- Facilitate responsiveness and flexibility to changes in the environment and consumer demands.

  - Reinforce the overall goals of the company e.g. a company who wishes to increase its customer responsiveness needs to adopt a flatter more decentralized organizational structure.

Advantages of centralization	Advantages of decentralization
Standard rules and policies enable swift decision making	Allows for more responsiveness to customer needs as no need to wait for a decision on a spur of the moment issue to be handed down from the top.
Allows for a holistic look at the firm as managers make decisions in the interest of the overall company	Allows for delegation and empowers employees to make decisions which are highly motivating

Motivation

Managers must have the ability to inspire their workers towards sustained efforts which are directed towards achieving company goals. Motivation is a force that makes people desire to achieve and work towards that achievement. Motivation is often spoke about as being inherent that is coming from within the individual – an internal drive but motivation can also be external, where factors outside such as pay, working conditions etc are applied to create the drive.

There are a number of motivational theorists. Here we will examine Maslow's Hierarchy of Needs, Mc Gregor's Theory X and Theory Y and Herzberg's Two Factor Theory/Hygiene Theory.

Maslow's Hierarchy of Needs

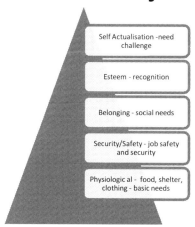

Need	Managers must provide the following to satisfy these needs
High order needs Self Actualization	Challenge, career growth, job enrichment, flexibility and autonomy
Esteem	Recognition, promotion, more responsibility
Lower level needs Belonging	Good relationships with colleagues, customer interaction
Security	Safety on the job
Physiological	Reasonable salary, comfort on the job, work breaks

📁 Maslow said that lower order needs must be satisfied before higher level needs can be met.
📁 Needs are satisfied in order. Once a need is satisfied it is no longer a motivator.
📁 Critics argue that not all persons have the same needs.
📁 Critics argue that persons may have several needs at once.

Herzberg's Two Factor Theory

Frederick Herzberg's theory centres around two factors as the name suggests – hygiene factors and motivators. Herzberg put forward that these two sets of factors influenced motivation in the workplace.

- **Hygiene Factors** – are those factors that do not motivate workers but do prevent dissatisfaction on the job. If good working conditions, adequate salary, good relationships with supervisors, job security and fair policies are absent they will produce dissatisfaction.

- **Motivators** – Herzberg concluded that motivators on the other hand once present did inspire people to work harder to achieve their targets and the organization's objectives. Motivators include recognition, opportunities for career growth, challenging and stimulating work, responsibility and achievement. Herzberg argued that once managers were able to create a working environment that provided these factors they would motivate employees.

Herzberg's motivators are very similar to Maslow's higher level needs. Critics of Herzberg's theory argue that it is natural for people to want to take credit for a job well done; hence they would identify achievement as a motivator. Also they note that a high level of job satisfaction does not always translate into more productivity.

Mc Gregor's Theory X and Theory Y

Mc Gregor's theory has been discussed earlier in this guide. Mc Gregor noted that there were two types of workers, those who disliked work and had to be micro managed and those who enjoyed challenging work with a degree of autonomy. Mc Gregor's theory implies that managers must use a variety of motivators as workers differ and as such require different types of motivators.

All the theories stress that a happy worker is a motivated worker and in turn a more productive worker. It must also be noted that there are a variety of techniques used to reward and motivate employees"

- Financial incentives – payment systems where workers must perceive that their financial rewards are fair and equitable to others in similar positions. Often performance reviews and appraisals are used to determine raises etc.

- Non financial incentives – include job satisfaction, job enrichment, job enlargement, opportunities for promotion, opportunities to participate in decision making.

Question:

Which type of worker are you X or Y?

Leadership

It is defined as guiding others towards the achievement of a goal or objective. It is necessary for employees to have a leader to guide them towards the achievement of a company's goals and objectives.

What makes a good leader?

- Effective communicator.

- Critical thinker.

- Good listener.

Are leaders born or can they be made?

There has been much debate over this question. There are some that argue that leadership traits are inherent to an individual i.e. people are born with and naturally possess the traits that make them a successful leader. This is often called the **trait theory.** There are critics of this theory that believe that managers and others can learn the skills required to make the effective leaders through skills training.

Leadership styles

Style	Characteristics	Disadvantages
Autocratic	Leader makes all the decisions	Not motivating for employees
	Micro managers workers – no autonomy	Leader may not have the expertise and know how to make sound decisions in every situation
	Top-down communication	
	Employees do not participate in decision making	
Democratic	Employees are encouraged to participate in decision making.	Consulting with staff on decisions is time consuming.
	Communication is two-way. Leader encourages feedback from employees.	Cannot be used when a snap decision is needed
	Workers are given all information needed to empower them to make decisions.	Some issues might be confidential and should not involve all members of staff
	Participation in decision making is a motivator.	

Laissez faire	Workers are given much freedom and autonomy when completing tasks.	Employees may lose direction and focus.
	Works well when employees are experts or a creative field.	The reduced role of the leader and lack of interpersonal relationships with leaders may lead to alienation and dissatisfaction.
	Can serve as a motivator for employees who value responsibility and autonomy.	Objectives may not be met as there is little guidance and direction.

Transformational	Involves leading people in an inspirational way.	It is based on the personality of the leader.
	Motivates workers,	Although these leaders are visionary, they may lack the detailed plans to achieve the vision.
	Inspires creativity and helps to smooth change management.	
	Encourages innovation e.g. Steve Jobs of Apple.	

Leadership roles

- Guide – assist employees in the achievement of their targets and giving them the resources to successfully complete their tasks.

- Direct – leaders should set clear objectives and goals for those that they lead.

- Counsel – a leader works closely with those on their team and aids them in their growth on the job, often working with them even when corrective action is needed.

- Coach and inspire – the leader should be like a cheerleader to those under his stewardship. Encouragement is a key source of motivation.

Manager vs. Leader

The question is often asked is a leader always a manager. The answer is a complex one. An effective manger should possess leadership ability to e successful. Leaders though are not necessarily managers but possess the traits and qualities that inspire others to follow their lead. These types of leaders are known as informal leaders.

Informal leaders – do not have formal power i.e. they are not managers or supervisors but are well respected and trusted by their colleagues. They may have specialist knowledge be an expert in their field; have a charismatic /likeable personality. Managers can use informal leaders to their benefit. When managers wish to implement change that may be resisted by the employees, taking the informal leader into their confidence and getting on him on the side of management, may be just what is required to lower resistance amongst employees. If it is endorsed by the informal leaders most other employees will buy into the new plans. All leaders, whether they are managers or informal leaders use power to lead others. Informal leaders may be more trusted and are more aware of organizational realities than formal leaders.

Manager
- analytical
- persistant
- structured
- authoritative
- has position power

Leader
- visionary
- innovative
- flexible
- passionate
- creative
- has personal power

Position Power - comes from formal position in the firm
- Legitimate power-based on job title and authority that comes with such e.g manger etc
- Reward power-comes from the ability to give people rewards for their positive actions
- Coercive power- managers may use their authority to punish to coerce/force workers to behave in a certain manner . This comes from the aility to hire and fire, suspend , dock pay etc.

Personal Power - comes from within and are traits of the leader
- Expert power - when a person is an expert in his field, extremely knowledgeale others turn to him for answers and so follow his lead.
- Referent power - some persons possess a personality that inspires others to respect , admire and wish to emulate and follow them.

Figure 7: Types of powers managers/leaders possess

Figure 8: Characteristics of Managers vs. Leaders

Teams –

A team is a group of two or more people who work together to accomplish a specific goal. Most modern day workplaces are now using teams in their organization structures.

- **Composition** – smaller teams (2 to 5) are more effective than larger teams (10 or more). Larger teams tend to have conflict, difficulty of co-ordination while smaller teams tend to have more effective communication and co-ordination.
    - o **Non participation** – as teams increase in size so does the opportunity for members to shun their responsibility. The larger teams tend to have more persons unwilling to share equally in the work load and do their part.
    - o **Diversity**-effective teams should have a diverse/varied composition of workers. There should be diversity in gender, ethnicity, expertise etc as this allows for the introduction of a variety of ideas and a mix of knowledge and skills. However, teams that are too diverse may experience a lot of conflict so the right balance must be struck.

- **Interaction** – the more team members interact and develop interpersonal relationships, the better the team functions as there is greater discussion, freer flow of ideas and increased co-operation. Through frequent interaction team members become loyal and committed to the team and its efforts.

- **Shared objectives** – The most effective teams agree on their goals and objectives. When there is a consensus on the direction and tasks a team should perform, members work better and the team is more cohesive.

Figure 9: Characteristics of an Effective Team

Stages of Team Development

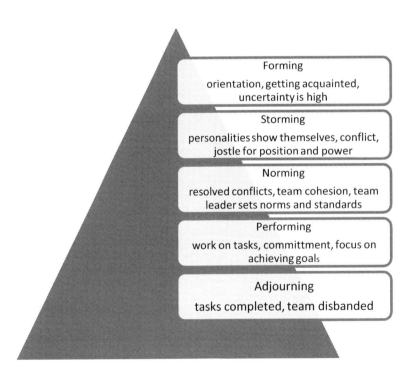

Team Conflict

It is often unavoidable that when two or more persons must collaborate that conflict will arise. Conflict as defined by Webster Dictionary is "struggle resulting from incompatible or opposing needs, drives, wishes or interests." The problem with conflict is that it may get in the way of the achievement of the team's goals and hence delay the firm from achieving its objectives.

Causes of Conflict

- Management style – when team leaders are autocratic in nature this may lead to lowered motivation and resistance, as other team members are not allowed to share their ideas and suggestions and as such rebel against or resist the directives given y the team leader.

- Competition for scarce resources – resources include money, time information and supplies. When individuals in a team or teams themselves must compete with others for these resources in order to complete their tasks, conflict will occur. To minimize this, managers must attempt to give all employees the tools to adequately perform their jobs.

- Communication – poor communication amongst team members will result in misinterpretations and misunderstandings. This can hinder trust which is important for effective team performance. It is important that team leaders communicate the same message to all members and that they encourage feedback so that misunderstanding and misinterpretation can be quickly remedied.

- Clash of personalities – a team is made up of different people each with his own unique personality, often personalities will clash. For instance a team member with a self confident, strong personality may e perceived as overbearing and obnoxious by others. Some members will just simply dislike the personalities of others in their team. This will cause conflicts as disagreements will become frequent. Personality differences are often difficult to solve.

Strategies to Manage Conflict

- Avoidance-those with the conflict can simply avoid each other or avoid discussing the issue. This works best when the issue is trivial such as the best time to meet etc and not critical to achieving the team's goals.

- Smoothing- differences are minimized so that the working relationship can be kept intact. It is also known as accommodating and involves much co-operation. Should only be used in less important situations and when harmony in the team is extremely important.

- Compromise – each conflicting view gives up some ground. Best when both parties have important points and suggestions are equally applicable or relevant. Some of one party's ideas get used and some of the other party's as well.

- Collaboration – working together to come up with one solution – merging into an overall solution.

- Confrontation- is a very assertive style where differences and grievances are aired. The goal is that once all is out in the open the work can move ahead. Often this just serves to further damage relationships among the members and disrupts the cohesion of the team.

Communication

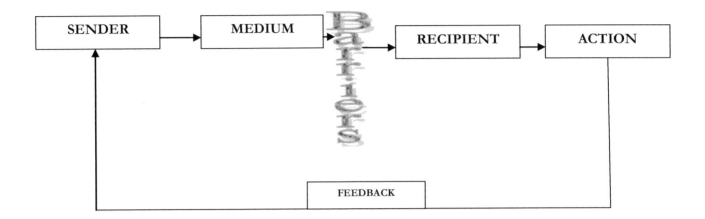

Communication is basically the exchange of information. The sender transmits the message by an appropriate medium (telephone, memo etc) to the recipient who acts based on what he received. Now effective communication must include feedback. It is in this way the sender knows if the correct message was sent and the recipient can clarify anything he might not have understood.

Barriers to Effective Communication

- Wrong medium used. E.g. if the message contains lots of technical details a video is an inappropriate medium, a document to which one can refer to would be more appropriate.

- Cultural bias– different ethnic groups may use different words to convey the same message. The same word has different meanings to different people, so this may result in misunderstanding the message. Also ethnic prejudices may cause persons not to limit or dismiss communication from other ethnic groups.

- Selective Perception – stereotyping and perceptions of people may influence how the message is received. If we perceive someone as a dishonest person we may ignore the message as we distrust them.

- Status differences – people at different levels of the organization may ignore or not communicate well. Managers may tend to not pay much attention to communication by lower level staff. Lower level staff may be intimidated to communicate with bosses.

- Physical noise – especially in manufacturing type environment may hinder effective communication.

Communication Methods/Media

Method	Advantages	Disadvantages
Oral – verbal: conversations, meetings, interviews, telephone	Direct, can be changed to suit the audience. Feedback is immediate. Non verbal clues/gestures can be used to help clarify message and meaning	Affected by physical noise, cannot refer to it later as there is no record, easily forgotten.
Written: memos, letters, bulletins, diagrams, minutes for meetings	Permanent record so it can be referred to at a later time. Easy to distribute through copies, more structured and organized.	Message is identical for each recipient despite recipient differences, no gestures to help clarify meaning and message, feedback is slower than oral communication. Costly for printing, time consuming to prepare.
Visual: video, pictures, graphs etc	Grabs attention, more interesting, useful in training and advertising	May miss details, interpretations by recipients may vary
Electronic; email, fax	Speed, near immediate feedback can be given, no geographical boundaries	Telecommunications can break down, workers can be overwhelmed with the sheer frequency and volume of electronic communication; reduces interpersonal relationships.

Reducing Barriers to Communication

- Choose the right medium.

- Keep the communication channel short, the fewer people between sender and recipient the better.

- Ensure feedback is given to correct any wrong or misleading information.

- Ensure there is trust between sender and recipient to prevent selective perception and attitude based barriers to communication.

- Try to communicate in the least noisy location as possible.

Lines of Communication

Communication flows throughout an organization in many ways:

Formal Communication Channel – this channel flows through the organization in the manner sanctioned by the managers and is facilitated by the organization's structure.

- Vertical – flows up and down. Downward is from management to employees and is often used for conveying direction, delegating tasks, performance feedback, and job instructions. Upward is from employees to management. This type of communication facilitates feedback and is used by employees to give suggestions and recommendations, air grievances, reports.

- Horizontal – is also known as lateral communication and occurs between departments or individuals on the same level of the organization hierarchy. E.g. Marketing Manager meets with the Finance Manager. It can be used to inform other departments, request support on projects, and is necessary in team based and matrix organization structures.

Types of formal communication networks

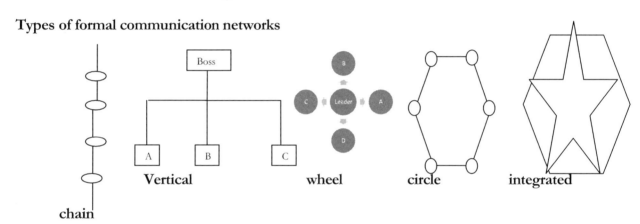

Communication network	Advantages	Disadvantages
Chain: hierarchy structure communication flows downwards only. Autocratic leader will like this style	Control over message. Useful in organizations that have highly sensitive/confidential information/products such as the army.	Does not encourage feedback, upward or horizontal communication. Workers may not feel motivated as suggestions go unheard and there is no participation. Inflexible and only a few messages can be sent at once.
Vertical: The boss communicates with his subordinates but the subordinates do not communicate with each other.	Useful in small departments.	No horizontal or upward communication, nor is feedback encouraged.

Wheel: Leader is at the centre and there is two way communication between leader and subordinates.	Feedback is encouraged, more flexible than vertical and chain networks. Moral is higher as well as two way communication is in effect.	No horizontal communication.
Circle: each person/department can only communicate with two others.	Two way communication, decentralized so morale is high.	No obvious leader and since communication is only with a select two an effective team environment is not created
Integrated: Full two way communication by all members. E.g. brainstorming sessions etc	Highly decentralized. High employee morale, flexible, can work well with complex problem solving	Time consuming

Informal communication – this type of communication occurs outside the formal structure and informal networks are formed because of personal relationships It is also known as the grapevine and links persons at all levels of the organization. It is office chatter and becomes more active in periods of change and uncertainty. The grapevine can be a source of misinformation and a hotbed of rumors. However, if managers study the grapevine and see who is networking with whom they can use it to disseminate key information and get support by targeting the grapevine's most influential persons.

Managing Change

Change is inevitable. Change in the context of a firm refers to moving from an old way of doing business to a new way of doing business, whether it is adopting new technology, adopting a new performance appraisal system.

Forces for Change – there are a number of factors/forces that may influence companies to change.

- Economic – as economic conditions change so too must businesses. The financial meltdown in the United States and the resulting economic recession has forced many businesses to reduce their workforce/the hours their employees work to make up for lagging sales.

- Technical – When companies automate and introduce new technology to make their businesses more efficient this too is a change in the status quo. Workers may have to be trained to effectively use the new technology/equipment.

- Demographic – as communities become more diverse and the type and number of resident change so too must businesses adapt to the needs of their new customers. For instance a small deli selling pizzas, subs and other high carbohydrate foods may face slowing sales when there is an influx of younger, health conscious persons moving into the neighborhood.

- Social – as societal norms, values and trends change so too must firms modify their products and services. As members of society become more environmentally conscious, companies have begun incorporating more environmentally friendly products into their lines.

- Legal – as government regulations are modified and implemented, firms must ensure that their companies are in compliance with them, this may require some changes.

Leading Change vs. Managing Change

Leading change involves having employees "buy into" the change, through persuasion, adoption of the change by the champion of the change, and in any way supporting the change. An effective leader will get others to follow his lead. Managing change refers to the management of the change process itself – implementation, training etc.

Implementing Change

The decision to change is an easy one but it is implementing the change that may prove most difficult for managers. Why? Simply because people in general fear what is new and different and so may resist changes. Resistance to change may be a result of:

- Fear – uncertainty of the unknown will often cause people to resist. Employees may not want to change because they are fearful of what the change will bring and so they resist. Will it mean longer hours and they wonder if they will be able to meet the requirements of the new way of doing business.

- Disrupted habits – employees resist because they have fallen into a routine and do not wish for it to be disrupted. They are comfortable and like the status quo.

- Loss of control – when change is introduced, employees are often a little bewildered and may no longer feel secure in their jobs or in their ability. This may also lead to their feeling that they lack purpose as they become more unsure of their worth in the new environment.

- Redistribution of workload – many times changes will include a shifting of job tasks and responsibilities. For instance if management decides to reduce its middle management layer, this may result in lower level workers having to assume more responsibility, something they may be unprepared/unwilling to do.

Overcoming Resistance to Change

- Participation – if workers are involved in the change management process they will resist less as they have had a say in the way the change will be implemented.

- Training – once workers are trained they will feel more confident and be less fearful that they are unable to perform in the new system.

- Communication – workers must be kept informed, this reduces anxiety, uncertainty and hence resistance.

- Coercion- unfortunately despite a manger's best efforts there might e a few workers who still resist the change. In these cases mangers ca use their formal power to force employees to change. For instance managers may dock pay or even fire those employees who refuse to operate in the changed system. This however may backfire as it reduces employee morale and hence productivity.

Human Resource Management

An organizational process that seeks to attract, develop and maintain an effective and efficient workforce. Management has over the years come to realize that its workforce, its human resources are as valuable if not more valuable than its other resources. No plan can be implemented, no god sold, no machinery run without people involved somehow. Human Resource Management (HRM) has a strategic role in the operation of any company. Let us take for example, that Firm PQR wishes to grow sales by offering superior customer service. HR managers must then attempt to evaluate the customer service skills of its current workforce, and offer retraining where needed. Additionally, any new hires must have that friendly service oriented attitude and unfortunately those unfriendly, rude employees who were not successfully retrained will have to be terminated.

Functions of Human Resource Management

> 💻 http://www.tutor2u.net/business/people /hrm_workforce_planning.htm
> 💻 (the spaces are underscores)

- **Recruitment** – is the process used to attract persons to apply for jobs at a firm. It also involves determining the requirements of the job, including the specific tasks and duties that must be performed by an individual who fills the post. This is known as a job description. A job specification is also required. A job specification is an outline of the qualifications such as education etc that a person must have to fill the said job. A specification outlines the minimum requirements for a job.

    o Companies recruit by advertising their job specifications and job descriptions to attract potential employees.

    Job description example

Job Description – Quick Study Co Ltd

Title: Sales and Marketing Executive

Reports to: Sales and Marketing Director,

Job role:

To plan and carry out direct marketing and sales activities, in order to maintain and develop sales.

Key responsibilities:

1. Maintain and develop a computerized customer database.
2. Plan and carry out direct marketing activities (principally direct mail).
3. Develop ideas and create offers for direct mail and marketing to major accounts by main market sector and Quick Study's products.
4. Respond to and follow up sales enquiries by post, telephone, and personal visits.
5. Maintain and develop existing and new customers.
6. Monitor and report on activities and provide relevant management information.
7. Carry out market research, competitor and customer surveys.
8. Manage the external marketing agency activities of telemarketing and research.

- **Selection** – the process of comparing applicants' qualifications and other attributes with what is required by the company. The person most suited to perform the job is chosen at this point.

  o Application forms, interviews, psychometric and psychological tests may be used in the selection process to wean out poor applicants and reveal the best match for the job.

- **Compensation** – the process of determining how much employees will be paid and any other benefits such as health care coverage that they might be entitled to. Compensation packages play a critical role in the attraction and retention of employees.

  o Job evaluations examine the value of jobs within a firm and help determine what compensation should be attached to those jobs.

  o Compensation should be equitable – in order to retain workers, HR managers should ensure that their pay scales are comparable to similar jobs in other companies in the industry, and that similar jobs within the company itself have similar compensation schemes.

  o Many firms are introducing pay for performance schemes in order to boost productivity. Workers are paid more based on their performance, maybe as a bonus. Often called incentive pay.

  o Benefits are essential to compensation plans. Benefits may include company cell phones and cars, health and dental insurance, on-site day care for workers, telecommuting as an option, etc. These intangible benefits are often the deciding factor for many employees when choosing a job.

- **Human Resource Development** – includes the firm's framework to support employees' development - their personal and organizational skills, knowledge, and abilities. Human Resource Development includes employee training, career development and planning, and coaching.

  o On the job training – a more experienced employee trains the new employee. It is cost effective but the older employee may pass on bad habits to the new employee and show him the easy way, which may not be the right way to do a job.

- Off the job training – as the name suggests this is more formal in nature and is conducted off of the firm's premises, perhaps at a training centre or conference room elsewhere. Though this is more costly, the trainers are professionals in their field and as such may be more effective than on the job training. However, employees may be unable to transfer their classroom experience to on the job.

- Computer based training – also known as e-training. This type of training delivers tutorials and modules via the Web. Employees log in and train through online tutorials and are tested online for mastery in the particular topic. As the cost of technology goes down this is quickly becoming a cost effective way for businesses to train their workers.

- **Performance management** – is the process used y firms to monitor the performance of their employees. The ultimate goal is to ensure that the right people are in the right jobs. Performance management tools include:

  - The performance appraisal – a tool used to evaluate the performance of workers by comparing their performance to specific criteria. This should be used to provide feedback to employees about their performance; it can also be used to determine raises, promotions, suspensions and terminations.

  - Performance appraisals can be prone to bias from stereotyping and rater bias.

Labour Management Relations/Employer-Employee Relations

"The study of labor-management relations (LMR) refers to the rules and policies which govern and organize employment, how these are established and implemented, and how they affect the needs and interests of employees and employers." (Von Otter, 2007)

Key Terms

- **Collective bargaining** – is a negotiation process where employees are collectively represented by their union, who bargains on behalf of them with their employers, often for better wages and working conditions.

- **Dispute settlement** – this occurs when an employee/employees take a grievance to their union, such as reduction of work hours, lay- offs etc and the union and the employer attempt to settle the disagreement/dispute.

  - The break down in collective bargaining and the inability y unions and employers to settle disputes can result in industrial action. Examples of industrial action include

    - Strikes – is stoppage of work by the majority of workers and is designed to force management to agree to the union's conditions.

    - Go slow - a protest in which employees demonstrate their dissatisfaction by carrying out their work slowly.

📁 Work –ins occur when workers continue to work despite a work stoppage order by management in situations where there will be a factory closure etc.

💻 **Visit my companion website www.managementofbusiness,webs.com . Go to Links, then Unit 1 Resources then view the resources on Trade Unions.**

Health and Safety in the Workplace

The health of workers and their safety on the job should be a primary concern of employers, after all ill and injured workers cannot be productive. There are government regulations that must be adhered to regarding health and safety on the job. Employers must ensure that

- Workers are educated about on the job safety.

- All facilities must be safety roofed, such as ensuring fire detectors, sprinklers, having an evacuation plan etc.

- Procedures to deal with safety complaints must be implemented and workers must be educated about those procedures.

Review Questions

1. Draw the communication process and discuss the barriers to communication and how they might be overcome.

2. Company Cheap Phone has implemented a time card system for its janitorial staff. This has not been received well by those concerned. The Office Manager overheard a member of the janitorial team – Susan complaining loudly, "Is this a prison? Why must they know when I come and go and when I go on break? Isn't it enough that my work gets done?" Discuss why Cheap Phone managers have implemented this new requirement and how they can overcome the employees' resistance.

3. Describe five main characteristics of Herzberg's Theory X and Theory Y workers.

4. The Scientific Management theory put forward by Frederick Taylor is of no relevance to contemporary workplaces. Discuss.

5. Leaders are born not made. Discuss.

6. Describe the five strategies team members can use to resolve conflict.

7. Think of the company you work or the institution you attend currently.

    a. Determine its organizational structure.

b. What are the advantages and disadvantages of that structure?

c. Would another organizational structure be more effective?

8. Consider the factors that motivate you. Which motivational theory would be best suited to spur on your motivation?

9. The office grapevine is a source of rumor, gossip and misinformation and can serve no useful purpose in a company. Discuss.

10. In light of the technological advancement and the changing face of organizations into more service oriented entities, the role of the union is obsolete. Discuss.

11. Research Elton Mayo's Hawthorne Experiments. What is referred to as the Hawthorne Effect?

12. Discuss THREE criticisms of the Human Relations Movement.

13. Define the Contingency Approach to management. Using an example explain how the Contingency Approach can be used in firms.

14. Consider the five functions of management below and define each one:

    a. planning

    b. organizing

    c. leading

    d. controlling

    e. staffing

15. Research FIVE of Fayol's Fourteen Principles and explain them.

16. Explain the following characteristics of the formal organization structure:

    a. accountability

    b. responsibility

    c. delegation

    d. authority

    e. line vs staff relationships

    f. chain of command

Business Finance and Accounting

A
ll businesses, no matter their size must manage their finances. After all, without adequate money management, the smallest of largest of companies will ultimately fail.

Why do businesses need capital?

- **Start up/venture capital** - www.businessdictionary.com defines start- up capital as "seed money", which is simply the money needed to begin one's business idea, to pay your first rent, licensing fees and all costs associated with starting a business.

- **Working capital** – the cash available to run the day to day operations of your company. Working capital is used to meet the short term obligations of the business, such as purchasing supplies, stock, paying rent and wages.

  o Current Assets – Current Liability = Working Capital

  o Current Assets – include cash or assets that are easily converted to cash e.g. cash, stock, accounts receivable

  o Current Liabilities – obligations that are expected to be paid by the business within a year e.g. short term loans, accounts payable.

- **Investment capital** – is money put back into the business to foster its growth and productive capacity. Investment capital may include investment in better machinery, a bigger plant.

Where do businesses get money from?

There are two main sources of finance for businesses.

- **Debt financing** – when companies borrow from lending institutions such as banks, they take on loans (which are a form of debt), which they repay over time with interest added. Debt financing can also be trade credit, where businesses are allowed to buy supplies and stock on credit, to be repaid at a later date often within the short term.

  o **Debentures** are a type of long term debt which is unsecured, meaning there is no collateral put up in the event that the debt is not repaid by the borrower. The two parties involved sign an agreement called an indenture.

  o **Bonds** – are issued for a period of a year or more and are a means of raising capital. There is a written agreement to repay. Governments, corporations and other institutions issue bonds. Some bonds do not pay interest but even if this is the case the principal amount is repaid.

Investors do not gain any ownership rights in the corporation but will e paid before a shareholder if the company was to close.

       o   **Short term debts** tend to e repaid within a year compared to long term debts.

- **Equity financing** - funds that are raised by a business in exchange for ownership in the company. Equity financing is often raised by issuing shares in the company. These investors may also have significant input into how the company is run and those with large investment may take an active role and sit on the Board of Directors. Unlike debt financing which must be repaid over time, equity financing does not have to be repaid. Equity also comes in the form of direct capital investment.

Debt vs. Equity Financing

The two types of financing options both have their advantages and disadvantages. What is important is that companies seek to have a reasonable debt to equity ratio, which ensures that they are not too heavily indebted as well as ensure that the ownership and control is not so severely diluted that the original owner no longer has power in his own firm.

Debt	Equity
Must be repaid with interest on a schedule, whether or not the business makes money.	Does not have to repaid
The original owner can retain control. Lending institutions are not interested in taking a share of the business.	Investors/shareholders can influence management decisions as they share ownership in the company.
Once the debt is repaid the lender has o further interaction or claim on the business.	Investors influence on the business only ends when they sell their shares.
It is often difficult for small businesses and new ventures to obtain debt financing.	

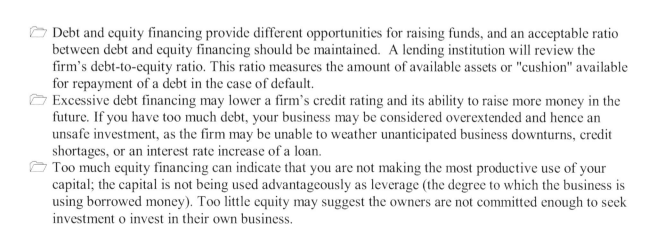

- Debt and equity financing provide different opportunities for raising funds, and an acceptable ratio between debt and equity financing should be maintained. A lending institution will review the firm's debt-to-equity ratio. This ratio measures the amount of available assets or "cushion" available for repayment of a debt in the case of default.
- Excessive debt financing may lower a firm's credit rating and its ability to raise more money in the future. If you have too much debt, your business may be considered overextended and hence an unsafe investment, as the firm may be unable to weather unanticipated business downturns, credit shortages, or an interest rate increase of a loan.
- Too much equity financing can indicate that you are not making the most productive use of your capital; the capital is not being used advantageously as leverage (the degree to which the business is using borrowed money). Too little equity may suggest the owners are not committed enough to seek investment o invest in their own business.

International Money and Capital Markets

Long term lending and borrowing markets are called capital markets, which are comprised of networks of banks and other financial institutions that offer debt financing.

Caribbean Development Bank: www.caribank.org

Founded in 1969, the Caribbean Development Bank (CDB has its headquarters in Barbados. Members of CDB include Caribbean territories and any non Caribbean states that are members of the United Nations. The CDB website states that:

Functions include:

- to assist the borrowing member countries to optimize the use of their resources, develop their economies and expand production and trade.
- to promote private and public investment, encourage the development of the financial upturn. in the region and facilitate business activity and expansion.
- to mobilize financial resources from both within and outside the region for development.
- to provide technical assistance to its regional borrowing members.
- to support regional and local financial institutions and a regional market for credit and savings.
- to support and stimulate the development of capital markets in the region.

Inter American Development Bank: www.iadb.org

This institution was established in 1959 and states that its function is to "to support the process of economic and social development in Latin America and the Caribbean, is the main source of multilateral financing in the region. The IDB Group provides solutions to development challenges by partnering with governments, companies and civil society organizations, thus reaching its clients ranging from central governments to city authorities and businesses."

The IDB has twenty-six member countries and provides grants and loans, the latter at competitive rates. It also offers technical assistance in the key areas of education, poverty reduction and agriculture.

International Monetary Fund

The IMF has 186 members and states that its mission is "working to foster global monetary cooperation, secure financial stability, facilitate international trade, promote high employment and sustainable economic growth, and reduce poverty around the world." Its main functions are

- **Lending to member countries** - provides loans to countries that have trouble meeting their international loan payments and are having difficulty sourcing alternative funding. It assists countries in stabilizing their balance of payments.
- **Surveillance** – The institution monitors the international monetary system and keeps track of economic developments on a national, regional, and global basis, consulting regularly with member countries and providing them with macroeconomic and financial policy advice.
- **Technical advice** – they implement structural adjustment programmes which are designed to assist borrowing countries in restructuring their economies such as their civil service, fiscal policies etc, so that they can successfully repay loans.

World Bank: http://web.worldbank.org

The World Bank provides technical and financial assistance to its 186 members. It is comprised of the International Bank for Reconstruction and Development (IBRD) and the International Development Association (IDA). The IBRD focuses on middle income and creditworthy poor countries, while IDA focuses on the poorest countries in the world. Together they provide low-interest loans, interest-free credits and grants to developing countries for investments in education, health, public administration, infrastructure, financial and private sector development, agriculture, and environmental and natural resource management.

The Stock Market

A public market for the buying and selling of a company's stocks at an agreed listed price.

- A stock is a small share in the company's ownership for which you pay. When you own stock and the company is profitable you receive a share of the profits in the form of dividends.
- Each stock gives you some voting power, so the more stock you own the greater your voting power and hence your influence on the company's decision.
- The two main types of stock are common and preferred.
  - Common stock - The basic stock a corporation issues. The common stocks are directly influenced by the success or failure of the company. Dividends to common stock holders are issued after those issued to preferred stock holders.
  - Preferred stock holders are paid a fixed dividend and so do not stand to profit as much as common stock holders if the company is extremely profitable, but they also do not stand to lose as much if the company does not do well.
- Stock split – often when a company has a high stock price and people are not buying the stock they give more stock for the money. If you own stock in a company that does a two for one stock split, you get double the amount of stock at the same value/price.

☐ Check out www.nyse.com to learn more about the New York Stock Exchange.
☐ Visit www.nasdaq.com to learn more about the NASDAQ.
☐ www.londonstockexchange.com to learn about London's Stock Market.
☐ www.ecseonline.com to learn about the Eastern Caribbean Securities Exchange.

💣※ Research some companies. Choose two companies you might like to invest in and follow their stocks over the next 3 months to see if you made a wise decision.
☐ Visit investopedia.com and trade stocks there in a virtual market.

Accounting

It is a necessity for businesses to maintain financial records. Records help firms track expenses and income, provide a record and ensure accountability. The American Accounting Association defines accounting as "the process of identifying, measuring and communicating economic information to permit informed judgments and decisions by users of the information."

Many persons use the financial information of a company including:

- Investors – want to assess a company's profitability and operational success.

- Employees – want to know about the company's profitability as the more profitable the greater job security they should have. Trade unions also review financial data and may use such to request pay increases for their members.

- Creditors – before issuing credit to a company, such as trade credit, creditors would review financial data to assess the ability of the business to pay its debt. This information is also required by lenders in financial institutions to determine if businesses are liquid enough to repay their loans.

- Government - may review financial information to determine the amount of tax that should be collected from the business which is often a percentage of profit or revenue.

- Public – the public is often interested in the activities of a business, perhaps in how much they give to charities, pay their CEOs etc.

Basic Accounting Concepts

- **Accounting Equation: Assets= Liabilities+Owners Equity**

  o **Assets – what a company owns**

    ▪ cash (money, cheques), Accounts Receivables, Inventory, Equipment

  o **Liabilities – what a company owes. E.g. Accounts Receivables**

  o **Equity**

    ▪ Retained earnings – income earned from operations

    ▪ Contributed or paid in capital – amount invested in a company by its owners.

- **Double Entry –** accounting concept that records the dual nature of transactions by recording the change in assets and the resulting change in liabilities or equity.

  o In a general ledger transactions are recorded in T accounts. Debits are recorded on the left, credits on the right.

Debit	Credit

ASSETS		LIABILITIES	
Debit	**Credit**	**Debit**	**Credit**
Increases	Decreases	Decreases	Increases

Example: The company buys $200 for the sale of goods.

```
          Bank                          Sales
  200     |                        |     200
          |                        |
```

- **Journal entry** – recording of an accounting transaction. The company buys $200 worth of supplies on credit.

Date	Description	Debit	Credit
11/12/2008	Supplies (asset increase)	200.00	
	Accounts Payable(liabilities increase)		200.00

Final Accounts
These are the accounts made up at the end of a company's financial year.

- The Trial Balance – consists of the net balances of all the company's ledgers at a particular date. This is a statement which is used to prepare the Final Account of Profit and Loss Account and a Balance Sheet.

T.Browne Company
Trial Balance
December 31, 2008

Account	Debit	Credit
Cash	6875	
Accounts Receivable	275	
Inventory	2225	
Accounts Payable		2050
Capital		7500
Revenue		1100
Expenses	1275	
	10650	**10650**

```
                Cash                                        Accounts Receivable

Sep  1   7550   |                               _____|_____
     17   400   |                               Sep 17   700  | Sep 25  425
     25   425   |                                             |
                |                                             |
Sep 15   1000   |                               _____|_____
     28   500   |                                    Bal. 275
_____|_____
```

Bal.   6825
┌──┐
│ 💻 www.moneyinstructor.com/lesson/trialbalance.asp   │
│ 💻 Visit the site for more information.   │
└──┘

•

┌──┐
│ 📂 The above are examples of how the balances are   │
│   calculated from the ledger accounts and placed into   │
│   the trial balance. The trial balance is then used to │
│   prepare the Income statement (Profit and Loss   │
│   Account and the Balance Sheet. Two Final Accounts.   │
└──┘

Profit and Loss Account/Income Statement

This is a Final Account that provides the Net Income of a company over a certain period. It shows the company's net profit/losses made over that period. The main elements of an Income Statement are:

- Net Sales/Revenue -compensation received for your product or services.

  - Cost of Goods Sold (COGS) – total value of goods sold to your customers in that time period. You have no COGS if you only provide a service.

  - Opening stock + Purchases made – Closing stock =COGS

  - Revenue – COGS = Gross Profit

- Operating Expenses – fixed expenses e.g. rent

- Other Income

- Other Expenses

The general template for calculating the company's net income/profit and loss:

Revenue – COGS=Gross Profit - Operating Expenses Operating Income + Other Income – Expenses=Earnings before taxes – income taxes = Net Income

T.P Browne Company
Profit & Loss Statement
January 1, 2007 to December, 2007

Sales	$200 000
Cost of Goods Sold	
Stock	$62 000
Purchases	$120 000
	$182 000
Less stock on hand	$60 000
Cost of goods sold	**$122 000**
Gross Profit	**$78 000**
Expenses	
Freight	$4 000
Commission	$10 000
Salary	$18 000
Office expenses	$4 000

Rent	$1 000
Insurance	$3 000
Depreciation	$1 000
Discounts allowed	$5 000
Bad debts	$2 000
Total expenses	**$48 000**
Net profit	**$30 000**

> http://www.va-interactive.com/cit/workshops/profitloss/index.htm
>
> **It is a long we address but gives you tutorials on preparing an Income statement. Well worth the visit!**

Balance Sheet

A snapshot of the company's assets and liabilities at a specific point in time.   The Balance Sheet is divided into:

- Assets – what your company owns.

    o   Fixed Assets – are permanent in nature e.g. land, building, equipment, vehicles.

    o   Current Assets – they are relatively liquid, i.e. easily converted to cash. –inventory, raw materials, cash, accounts receivables.

    o   Assets=Liabilities + Owner's Equity

- Liabilities – anything a company owes.

    o   Current Liabilities – are short term in nature and must be paid within one year. E.g. creditors, short term loans.

    o   Long term liabilities – is a debt that is due in a time frame that is longer than one year.

- Owner's Equity – is the remaining assets after liabilities are paid. It is the owner's claim on the business. Owner's Equity = Assets – Liabilities.

Tamu Browne Ltd	
Balance Sheet as at December 2012	**$**
Assets	
Cash in Bank	23000
Accounts Receivables	7000
Inventory	5000
Total Current Assets	**35000**
Machinery	9600
Total Assets	**44600**
Liabilities	
Accounts Payable	3600
Loans	3000
Total Liabilities	**6600**
Equity	
Share Capital	25000
Retained Earnings	3000
Net Profit	10000
Total Liabilities and Equity	**44600**

> 💻 Visit www.tutor2u.net and put "balance sheet" into the search
> box to find numerous resources.

Depreciation

Is an expense that reduces the value of a fixed asset. Most fixed assets lose their value over time die to wear and tear and also may become obsolete as new models come on the market. Accounts are adjusted to show such depreciation. Depreciation reduces the company's earnings.

Straight Line Depreciation – This is the simplest method to calculate depreciation. It is calculated using the following formula: **Purchase price – salvage value/estimated useful life of the asset.**

Example: The company purchases a computer for $2000. A reseller has told you that when the company wants to get rid of the computer he will buy it for $400 and resell it for parts. The Information Technology Manager estimates that the computer will become obsolete in 4 years. What are the computer's depreciation charges?

Answer: (2000-400)/4 = 1600/4= $400 per year

Declining Balance/Reducing Balance Method/Accelerated Balance Method

This method is called reducing balance because the highest depreciation charges are found in the earlier life of the asset, and the gets less or reduces as the asset ages.

Example: Company A purchased van for $40,000 and it is estimated that 20% depreciation rate will be used.

YEAR 1 - $ 40,000 (purchase price)

- less <u>$8,000</u> (20% of $40,000) *Provision for Depreciation Year 1*
  - $ 32,000 (asset value at the end of year 1)

YEAR 2 - $ 32,000 (asset value at the end of year 1)

- less <u>$ 6400</u> (20% of $32,000) *Provision for Depreciation Year 2*

  - $ 25,600 (asset value at the end of year 2)

YEAR 3 - $ 25,600 (asset value at the end of year 2)

- less <u>$5,120</u> (20% of $25,600) *Provision for Depreciation Year 3*

  - $20,480 (asset value at the end of year 3)

YEAR 4 - $ 20,480 (asset value at the end of year 3)

- less <u>$4,096</u> (20% of $20,480) *Provision for Depreciation Year 4*

  - $16,384 (asset value at the end of year 4) and so on until the asset has no value.

> 💻 Visit Google books and enter "reducing balance depreciation + worked example" for tons of questions and information on depreciation.

Write your notes here

_____

_____

_____

_____

_____

_____

_____

Stock Valuation

There are three accounting methods companies can use to determine the value of their inventory.

- LIFO – Last in First Out method assumes that the last unit purchased is the first unit to be sold.

- FIFO – First in First Out – assumes the first unit purchased is the first unit sold.

- Weighted Average – is simplest as it merely calculates the average cost of stock purchased over the period and applies that to the ending inventory.

- Stock valuation is used to compute the COGS for the Income Statement. Depending on which method is used it affects the company's net income figure.

Example: T.P. Browne Company has an opening stock of 1000 units at $8 per unit.

Month	Purchases	Unit cost
January	1000	$10
February	1000	$12
March	1000	$15
Total	3000	

The Ending inventory is the (1000 opening stock + purchases of 3000 units) – units sold of 3000. (1000+3000) – 3000 = 1000 units.

LIFO: The last amount purchased was the opening stock of 1000 at $8 thus the ending stock is $8000.

FIFO: Ending stock in this case is the last amount bought since we sell the first ones thus the ending stock is 1000 at $15 = $15000

Weighted Average: The average stock is computed: (1000x$8) + (1000x$10) + (1000x$12) + (1000x$15)/4000 =$8000+$10,000+$12,000+$15,000/4000 =45000/4000 = $11.25

Thus the ending inventory is 1000x$11.25 = $11,250.

Now let us look at how the different stock valuation methods affect the Income Statement.

T.P. Browne Company sold their 3000 units to customers at $30 each.

Method	LIFO	FIFO	Weighted Average
Sales (3000x30)	**90,000**	**90,000**	**90,000**
Beginning inventory (1000x8)	8000	8000	8000
Purchases (10,000+12,000+15,000)	37,000	37,000	37,000
Ending inventory	8,000	15,000	11,250
COGS	**37,000**	**30,000**	**33,750**
Expenses	7500	7500	7500
Net Income	**45,500**	**52,500**	**48,750**

Cash Flow statements

The cash flow statement reports the sources and uses of cash during the period under review. It provides information on the liquidity of the firm and it also indicates the amount, timing and probability of future cash flows. There are two methods to prepare the statement – direct and indirect methods.

- **Direct Method -** it looks at the cash receipts and payouts and is simpler than the indirect method.

  o **You take your cash receipts from customers and deduct**

    ▪ **Cash paid for stock**

    ▪ **Cash paid to employees – wages etc**

    ▪ **Cash paid for operating expenses**

    ▪ **Taxes**

    ▪ **Interest**

  o **Equals net cash.**

T.P. Browne Company

Cash flow statement for January 2009

Cash receipts

Cash Sales	200,000
Debtors payments	50,000
Loan received	100,000
Total cash receipts	**350,000**

Cash payments

Rent	10,000
Wages	75,000
Utilities	8,000
Advertising	110,000

Purchase of fixed assets	95,000
Total cash payments	**298,000**
Net cash flow (total receipts- total payments)	**52,000**
Opening cash balance – receipts were less than payments the previous month hence a negative balance.	**(10,000)**
Closing cash balance (will be next month's opening balance)	**$42,000**

- **The Indirect Method** – uses the net income figure from the income statement and reverse entries to income and expense accounts that do not involve cash, and it shows the change in net working capital. Entries that do not represent cash flows could include income you have earned but not yet received, amortization of prepaid expenses, accrued expenses, and depreciation.

- **Net income from the income statement**

  o **Deduct entries to receipts that do not include cash**

  o **Plus expenses that do not represent cash flow**

- **Equals cash flow before changes in working capital**

  o **Plus or minus the change in working capital**

    ▪ An increase in current assets (excluding cash and cash equivalents) would be shown as a negative figure because it reduced the cash balance.
    ▪ A decrease in current assets would be shown as a positive figure.
    ▪ An increase in current liabilities excluding short-term debt would be shown as a positive figure since more debt means that less cash was paid out.
    ▪ A decrease in current liabilities would be shown as a negative figure, because cash was spent in order to reduce liabilities/debt.

- **The net effect is your cash flow figure.**

It is important that a firm monitor its cash flow as insufficient cash flow may lead to the following situations:

  ▪ Inability to pay creditors, which may result in loss of discounts, added interest costs and loss of goodwill with the firm's suppliers.

- Inability to pay employees which would result in low employee morale and workers leaving the company.

- Inability to expand the firm including the purchasing of new equipment to maintain or increase output.

- Negative cash flows can be solved by reducing expenditure, cutting costs, obtaining cheaper materials, rent or lease equipment instead of purchasing, obtain an overdraft or short term loan and reduce the time the company gives debtors to repay.

> 🖥 Visit www.managementofbusiness.webs.com visit Unit 1 Resources on the Links page and explore the wealth of resources there.

Challenge for you!
Use the space below to create your own personal cash flow statement. Where is your money going?

Budgeting

A budget is a financial plan for the future concerning the revenues/costs of the business.

Uses of a budget
- Controls income and expenditure.
- Helps monitor performance.
- Provides direction for staff.
- Establish priorities and targets.

Effective budgets should include the investigation of variances. Variances are the differences between actual spending or revenues and budgeted amounts. Any unapproved variances should be investigated.

Limitations of budgets
- They can lead to centralization of decision making.
- Time consuming.
- May demoralize workers if they are uninvolved in the budgeting process.
- If the data used is not timely, relevant or accurate, unrealistic budgets may be created.

Budgetary control

- **Variance analysis** – as discussed earlier any deviations from the budget must be approved or accounted for. This leads to stricter adherence to the budget.

- **Responsibility accounting** – this technique creates cost/revenue centres. For instance a large multinational may make each of its branches or even departments a cost or revenue centre. The branch or department would have its own budget instead of being lumped with the firm's overall budget. This makes control easier.

- **Zero based budgeting** – this starts each cash budgeting period afresh. No budgets are set based on historical data. Instead each activity for which money is required must be justified and approved.

Investment Analysis

When companies undertake investment, it is important that they be able to determine how successful their investment has been. The use of investment ratios can allow firms to measure the profitability of the investments they make. These ratios guide firms in making decisions whether to invest in a project or not.

Pay-back period – determines the amount of time required for a company to recoup/make back the money it spent on the investment.

- It is easy to calculate.

- It ignores what occurs after the pay-back period.

- It does not take into account the time value of money (the worth of a dollar in the future. For instance what a dollar can buy now may not be what a dollar can buy tomorrow)

- **Calculation:** The cost of the project/annual cash inflows. E.g. If a project costs $200,000 and the projected annual return on the project is expected to be $40,000. What is the pay-back period?

  - 200,000/40,000 = 5 years. The firm will get back its investment in the fifth year of the project. If the company is trying to decide on which project to invest in it should choose the one with the shortest pay-back period.

Average Rate of Return – the ratio of average cash received to the amount of funds invested. It looks at the expected net cash flows of the investment project and then measures the average net return each year as a percentage of the initial cost of the investment.

- It shows the profitability of the investment.

- Does not take into account the time value of money nor the risk involved in the investment.

Calculation:

Year	1	2	3	4	5
Cash flow	40,000	50,000	55,000	60,000	65,000

T.P. Browne Company purchased a machine for $200,000 and the expected cash returns are above. Calculate the average rate of return.

- Calculate total return = 40,000+50,000+55,000+60,000+65,000= $270,000

- Calculate the net return = 270,000 – 200,000 = $70,000

- Calculate average return = 70,000/5 = $14,000 per year

- Calculate average rate of return = Net return per annum/initial cost x 100=14000/200000 x100=7% This means that for every dollar invested the firm gets an average 7 cents per year.

Net Present Value – (NPV) takes into account the time value of money. To determine the NPV of a set of cash flows, you must use an interest rate that defines the current time value of money. Each firm will decide what that interest rate is. To determine which project to choose the firm will choose the highest NPV projects as they are the ones that will provide the most profit. If the project only represents costs, then you want to choose the project with an NPV closest to zero, but not less than zero.

- Takes into account the time value of money and so is good for appraising long term projects.

- It is difficult to determine what discount rate should be used/the percentage.

Calculation: You will be given a factor table to locate the discount factors for the particular rate or they will be given to you. In a tale the discount factor is found at the interaction of the year and the percentage.

Year	Factor for 15%	Cash flows	Present Value
0	1.000	-50,000	-50,000
1	.8696	20,000	17392
2	.7561	25,000	18903
3	.6575	20,000	13150
4	.5718	30,000	17154
NPV			**16599**

🖳 Visit www.cliffsnotes.com and enter "net present value" for more information.

Internal Rate of Return (IRR)

Is the discount rate that generates a zero net present value for a series of future cash flows. This means that IRR is the rate of return that makes the sum of the present value of future cash flows and the final market value of a project (or an investment) equal to its current value.

The Internal Rate of Return is the opposite side of the coin of NPV, where NPV is the discounted value of a stream of cash flows, generated from an investment, the IRR calculates the rate of return showing the discount rate, below which an investment results in a positive NPV. IRR is expressed as a percentage.

- It is simple as a project will be accepted if its Internal Rate of Return exceeds the cost of capital and rejected if this IRR is less than the cost of capital.
- IRR neglects the size of the project and assumes that cash flows are reinvested at a constant rate.
- It considers the time value of money.

Example: A project costing $7,500 is expected to return $2,000 per year for five years, or $10,000 in total. The IRR calculated for the project would be 10 percent. If your cost of borrowing for the project is less than 10 percent, the project may be worthwhile. If the cost of borrowing is 10 percent or greater, it won't make sense to do the project (at least from a financial perspective) because, at best, you'll be breaking even.

- Calculate the number to look up in the present value tables. $7500/2000 = 3.8$
- Then use the present value tables and look at the row corresponding to the number of years the (in this case, five). Look across the rows until you find the number that is closest to the result you found (3.8). Then look at the top of the column in which the closest number was found, to see the interest rate that is your IRR (in this case, 10 percent).
- In this case if it costs the company 10% or more to borrow the investment money, the project should be abandoned. If the cost of capital is less than 10%, the project should be undertaken.

Discuss below the advantages and disadvantages of each type of investment appraisal method. Which would you use if you were the CEO of a casino wanting to invest in one of three types of new arcade games? Why?

References

Von Otter, C. (2007). Labor-management relations. In G. Ritzer (Ed.), *Blackwell encyclopedia of sociology*. Blackwell Publishing. Blackwell Reference Online. Retrieved June 13, 2007, from http://www.blackwellreference.com/subscriber/book?id=g9781405124331_9781405124331.

Stimpson Peter (2002) Business Studies: AS and A Level Student's Coursebook (Cambridge International Examinations)

Daft Richard L. (2005) The New Era of Management. International Student Edition. Thomson South-Western.

Made in the USA
Middletown, DE
27 September 2022

11311621R00040